CLEVELAND SPORTS TRIVIA QUIZ

Tim Long

GRAY & COMPANY, PUBLISHERS • CLEVELAND

© 1999 by Tim Long

Gray & Company, Publishers
1588 E. 40th Street
Cleveland, OH 44103
(216) 431-2665
www.grayco.com

Library of Congress Cataloging-in-Publication Data
Long, Tim
Cleveland sports trivia quizbook / by Tim Long.
1. Sports—Ohio—Cleveland—Miscellanea. 2.
Sports—Ohio—Cleveland—History. I. Title.

GV584.5.C58 L66 1999
796'.09771'32—dc21   99-6710

ISBN 1-886228-29-9

Printed in the United States of America

10 9 8 7 6 5 4 3 2 1

ACKNOWLEDGEMENTS

Special thanks to the following people for their help with this book:

Al "Bubba" Baker, former Browns defensive lineman; WERE 1300 AM radio talk show host

Les Levine, Cablevision talk show host and sports personality

John Tidyman, friend and author of the *Cleveland Golfer's Bible*

Bob Dolgan, *The Plain Dealer*

Dick Goddard

Curtis Danberg, Cleveland Indians

Bob Frantz, WTAM 1100 AM sports talk

John Ferchill, Cleveland Sports Commission; involved with the Ohio Games; real estate developer

Bill Needle, Cablevision sports personality; formerly WKNR talk host

Brian Brakeman, Ohio high school wrestling expert; *The Brakeman Report*

Russ Schneider

Terry Pluto, the *Akron Beacon Journal*

Pat Mazoh, Bertman Foods

Doug Dieken

Kendall Lewis, WKNR 1220

Chris Wenzler, John Carroll University Sports Information Director

William Reith, Alcazar Fencing Club

Hal Lebovitz, *News Herald* and *Lorain Morning Journal*

Joe Horrigan, Curator, Pro Football Hall of Fame, Canton, Ohio

? ?

1. What was the name of the street that ran alongside Cleveland Municipal Stadium?

2. In 1955, whom did *Plain Dealer* sportswriter Harry Jones call "the heir apparent to Feller's throne"?

3. Browns defensive end Joe Jones (1970–1973 and 1975–1978) was known as Joe "_____" Jones. Fill in the blank.

4. What annual event for amateur athletes did the Cleveland Sports Commission establish in 1992?

5. Who said "Don't look back, something might be gaining on you" (1948)?

1. *Boudreau Boulevard, named in honor of Tribe shortstop and player-manager, Lou Boudreau.*

2. *Herb Score, then a rookie pitching sensation.*

3. *Turkey.*

4. *The Ohio Games.*

5. *Indians pitcher Leroy "Satchel" Paige.*

? ?

6. Who was the first player taken by the Cleveland Browns in the 1999 NFL college draft on April 17, 1999?

7. Now a sports-talk host on WTAM 1100, Mike Trivisonno made a name for himself as a regular caller to Cleveland sports-talk shows in the 1970s and 1980s. What nickname did he use?

8. What Cleveland-area high-school baseball teams have won Ohio high-school state baseball championships?

9. Who was the Browns' starting quarterback in their first pro game?

10. Which Cavaliers guard went on to coach the team and became the win-ningest NBA coach, while coaching the Atlanta Hawks?

6. *Quarterback Tim Couch of the University of Kentucky.*

7. *"Mr. Know-it-All."*

8. *Seven schools have won the Division I (formerly Class AAA) title: Shaw High School (1944, 1968), Lincoln High School (1946), Cleveland Heights High School (1947), South High School (1961), Euclid High School (1963, 1982), Shaker Heights High School (1965, 1976), and Wickcliffe High School (1974). Holy Name High School won the Class AA championship in 1981, and Mayfield won the Class B title in 1934.*

9. *Cliff Lewis of Lakewood (Ohio) High School and Duke University opened against the Miami Seahawks in the Browns' first-ever pro game in the All America Football Conference. (Otto Graham is not a bad guess, but he joined the Browns late in the 1946 season and was still learning the plays.)*

10. *Lenny Wilkens.*

???

11. The Shoremen are battling the Warriors in a Southwestern Conference gridiron contest. Who is playing?

12. Who writes the wildlife–outdoors column for the *Plain Dealer*?

13. What Cleveland team defeated Pele and his World Cup champion Santos soccer team (Brazil) at Cleveland Stadium on July 10, 1968?

14. What two Cleveland-area high schools have made consecutive appearances in the Ohio high-school state baseball championship game?

15. Where is the Greater Cleveland Slo-Pitch Softball Hall of Fame?

11. *Avon Lake and Fairview.*

12. *D'Arcy Egan.*

13. *The Cleveland Stokers of the North American Soccer League. It was the first loss handed the World Cup champs on their 1968 U.S. tour.*

14. *The Euclid Panthers (Division I, 1978 and 1979) and the Rocky River Pirates (Division II, 1998 and 1999).*

15. *East 222nd Street in Euclid, Ohio. (It was originally located at Softball World, on West 130th Street in Parma.)*

? ?

16. What is the seating capacity for the new Cleveland Browns football stadium?

17. In the first major boxing match in Cleveland since 1931, whom did Muhammad Ali defeat in 15 rounds at the Richfield Coliseum on March 24, 1975?

18. What was the name of the Cleveland Indians' former spring training site in Tucson, Arizona?

19. Who was the Cleveland Browns' first NFL draft pick in the 1950 college draft?

20. Who holds the Cavaliers' record for points-per-game scoring average?

16. 72,300.

17. Chuck Wepner, a New Jersey liquor salesman turned pro boxer, also known as the "Bayonne Bleeder."

18. Hi Corbett Field.

19. Ken Carpenter, a halfback from Oregon State University.

20. Lloyd "World B." Free at 23 points per game.

???

21. Randall Park Mall sits atop the remains of what sixty-year-old sporting institution?

22. Name the 1988 farcical movie that portrayed the Cleveland Indians as a team of misfits that won the American League pennant.

23. What two Cleveland-area high-school sports teams are called the Blue Devils?

24. What Youngstown, Ohio, professional boxer went by the name "Boom-Boom"?

25. What former Cleveland Indian outfielder played major league baseball in five decades—the 1940s, '50s, '60s, '70s, and '80s?

21. *The Randall Park Race Track. The track was closed in 1969 and demolished in 1973.*

22. Major League *starred Tom Beringer, Rene Russo, Corbin Bernsen, Wesley Snipes, and Charlie Sheen.*

23. *Brunswick and Independence.*

24. *Ray Mancini.*

25. *Minnie Minoso, who played for Cleveland in 1949; for the Chicago White Sox and Cleveland in the 1950s; the White Sox, St. Louis Cardinals, and Washington Senators in the 1960s; three games for the White Sox in the 1970s; and two games for the White Sox in 1980.*

26. What innovation was introduced in Cleveland on August 18, 1962, as part of the NFL preseason schedule?

27. Indians outfielder Paul Dade (1977–1979), Cavalier Milos Babic (briefly, in the 1990-91 season), and Crunch goalie Otto Orf (1989–1999) all did what?

28. What nickname was given to the 1940 Indians team?

29. Name the Pro Football Hall of Fame player from Stow, Ohio, whose nickname was "the lawn mower" (describing his low-to-the-ground style of running).

30. What Clevelander won gold medals in track and field in the 1948 and 1952 Olympic Games?

26. *The pro football double header. Before 77,683 fans on that Saturday night, the Detroit Lions beat the Dallas Cowboys 35–24 in the first game, and the Browns defeated the Pittsburgh Steelers 33–10 in the nightcap.*

27. *Wore the uniform number "00."*

28. *The "Crybabies," because of their complaints over the manner in which the team manager, Oscar Vitt, handled the players.*

29. *Larry Csonka.*

30. *W. Harrison Dillard, who won the 100-meter event in 1948 and finished first with the 4x100-meter team in 1948 and 1952.*

??

31. What local Cleveland golf course did Arnold Palmer call home when he served in the U.S. Coast Guard in the early 1950s?

32. Who was the last Indians pitcher to win 20 games or more in a season?

33. Who was the first player taken by the new Cleveland Browns in the February 9, 1999, expansion draft?

34. What type of indoor recreational facility was first established in downtown Cleveland in 1872, in response to the popularity of a certain pasttime among the city's German population?

35. What occasion prompted the 1997 Indians team to hike up their socks (and thereby, many claim, inspire their drive to the playoffs that season)?

31. *Pine Ridge Country Club in Willoughby (now a public golf course).*

32. *In 1972, Gaylord Perry won 24 games to lead the American League.*

33. *Jim Pyne, an offensive lineman from the Detroit Lions.*

34. *Cleveland's first bowling alley, which was opened on Bank Street (now West 6th Street).*

35. *First baseman Jim Thome's birthday.*

???

36. Cleveland businessman Al Lerner purchased the expansion Cleveland Browns football franchise on September 8, 1998, for what price?

37. Which Cuyahoga County commissioner spearheaded a 1984 effort to raise property taxes to fund a domed stadium in Cleveland?

38. How many players hit a home run into the center-field bleachers at Cleveland's Municipal Stadium, home of the Indians from 1932 to 1993?

39. What Browns player was nicknamed "Zeus"?

40. What affectionate term was used to describe the Cleveland Cavaliers' surprising performance in the 1976 NBA playoffs?

36. *$530 million.*

37. *Vincent C. Campanella.*

38. *No batter ever reached the old Stadium bleachers and none ever will.*

39. *Orlando Brown (1994–1995), who again joined the Browns as a free agent in the 1999 season.*

40. *The Miracle of Richfield.*

??

41. What club was founded on February 1, 1908?

42. For whom did the Indians host a "Welcome Back" night on June 11, 1976, when the Chicago White Sox came to town?

43. For what is Dwight Clark, current vice president of Football Operations for the Cleveland Browns and former San Francisco 49er, most remembered?

44. By what nickname is sports memorabilia expert and former radio sports-talk host Geoff Sindelar known?

45. Give at least one popular legend surrounding the Cleveland Indians' 1980 Rookie of the Year, "Super Joe" Charboneau.

41. The Cleveland Athletic Club. (It was the second club to be called the CAC, the first having disbanded in the 1890s.)

42. Bill Veeck, the flamboyant owner of the Indians from 1946 to 1949, who had sponsored many special events for the fans.

43. Catching the famous touchdown pass from quarterback Joe Montana in the 1982 NFC championship game against the Dallas Cowboys that put the 49ers in the Super Bowl. The play is known simply as "The Catch."

44. The Professor.

45. Here are four: 1) He pulled one of his own teeth; 2) He opened a beer bottle using one of his eye sockets as an opener; 3) Because of a broken nose, he could drink beverages through his nose using a straw; 4) Charboneau once sewed up a cut with fishing line.

??

46. Who was the first football coach to win a national collegiate championship and an NFL championship?

47. The first Revco-Cleveland Marathon was run in which northern Ohio city in 1976?

48. Indians outfielder Carroll Hardy (1958–1960) played what other professional sport in 1955 before coming to the Indians?

49. The late 1970s and early 1980s saw the Browns feature two running backs with the same letters in their last names and the same numerals in their uniform numbers. Who were they?

50. What Cleveland Cavaliers player won the NBA All-Star Game long distance shooting contest in 1994?

46. Paul Brown coached Ohio State University to the national collegiate championship in 1942 and led the Browns to an NFL title in 1950.

47. Hudson, Ohio. (That first race attracted 250 runners.)

48. Football, for the San Francisco 49ers.

49. Halfback Greg Pruitt, #34; and fullback Mike Pruitt, #43.

50. Mark Price.

51. The Cleveland Metroparks Rocky River Reservation Golf Course No.1 and No. 2 are better known by what nicknames?

52. What famous Indians outfielder was known as the "Gray Eagle"?

53. Who was the Cleveland Browns' mascot during their days in the All-America Football Conference, from 1946 to 1949?

54. Cleveland's Harold T. Clark Tennis Courts have been located at what two places?

55. How many radio broadcast partners did Herb Score have between 1968 and 1997? Name them.

51. "Big Met" and "Little Met."

52. Tris Speaker (1916–1926) received this nickname due to his graying hair and his
    ability to patrol center field like an eagle.

53. The Browns employed Tommy Flynn, a dwarf, as their team mascot.

54. Ambler Park in Cleveland Heights and at the east end of the Municipal Parking Lot
    along the East Shoreway.

55. Six: Bob Neal, 1968–1972; Joe Tait, 1973–1979; Nev Chandler, 1980–1984; Steve
    Lamar, 1985–1987; Paul Olden, 1988–1989; Tom Hamilton, 1990–1997.

CLEVELAND SPORTS TRIVIA QUIZ

? ?

56. In 1968, wide receiver Tommy McDonald was the last Browns player to do what?

57. What Cleveland sportswriter was known for his *Plain Dealer* column, "Off the Cuff"?

58. Where was the first Cleveland Open professional golf tournament played?

59. What former Browns receiver has the Ohio license plate "Mr. Glue"?

60. When the Cleveland Cavaliers were named in 1970 by a fan vote, what were the four other names offered for consideration?

56. *Play without a protective face mask.*

57. *Chuck Heaton.*

58. *Beechmont Country Club in Orange Village.*

59. *Dante Lavelli, whose nickname "Gluefingers" was given because of his pass-catching ability.*

60. *The Towers, Presidents, Jays, and Foresters.*

CLEVELAND SPORTS TRIVIA QUIZ

61. Who was the Cleveland Barons hockey team's player-coach from 1962 to 1968?

62. What are the most runs scored by the Cleveland Indians in a game?

63. How did the football term "taxi squad" originate?

64. The Pirates are playing the Bruins in high-school baseball. What two schools are on the diamond?

65. What New York City high-school senior was the Indians' first pick in the 1991 amateur baseball draft?

61. *Fred Glover, whose Barons career stretched from 1953 to 1968.*

62. *Twenty-seven, against the Boston Red Sox on July 7, 1923.*

63. *The Cleveland Browns' first owner, Arthur "Mickey" McBride, kept non-roster players in town by giving them jobs as drivers for his taxi company. If injuries hit the team, replacements were nearby driving taxis.*

64. *Rocky River and Padua.*

65. *Outfielder Manny Ramirez.*

66. How did former Browns quarterback Bernie Kosar earn his Super Bowl ring?

67. What well-known athlete/actor set the world 150-yard-backstroke record at the Cleveland Athletic Club (CAC) pool in 1992?

68. What year was Indians mascot Slider's first season?

69. Who replaced Don Cockroft in 1981 after 12 years as the Browns' place-kicker?

70. What Clevelander won four gold medals in the 1936 Olympic Games in Berlin, Germany?

66. *As a backup quarterback with the Dallas Cowboys in the 1993 season, after being released by the Browns.*

67. *Johnny Weissmueller, at the National Swimming Championships.*

68. *1991.*

69. *Dave Jacobs, a non-drafted free-agent kicker from Syracuse University. Jacobs did not last through the 1981 season.*

70. *Jesse Owens finished first in the 100-meter dash, the 200-meter dash, and the long jump, and was a member of the first-place 400-meter-relay team.*

71. How long is the Medic Grand Prix of Cleveland auto race (formerly the Budweiser-Cleveland 500 Grand Prix)?

72. Most fans remember Indians slugger Rocky Colavito's uniform number as 6. What two other numbers did he wear in his Tribe career?

73. What did the 1948 Cleveland Browns do three times within eight days?

74. What Cleveland sports announcer has done play-by-play for three Cleveland sports teams that have gone out of business?

75. For what professional Cleveland sports team does Zoran Karic play?

71. *500 kilometers.*

72. *Number 38, from 1955 to 57; and 21, when he returned to the Indians in 1965. (He wore number 6 as a player in 1958–1959 and again as a coach from 1973 to 1978.)*

73. *The Browns accomplished the near impossible in November 1948—they won three AAFC games in one week. On Sunday, November 21, they beat the New York Yankees 34–21 in New York. On Thanksgiving Day, November 25, they beat the Los Angeles Dons 31–14 in Los Angeles, and on Sunday, November 28, they topped the San Francisco 49ers 31–28 in San Francisco.*

74. *Les Levine owns this dubious distinction. He called the action for the Competitors (indoor soccer), the Crusaders (hockey), and the Thunderbolts (indoor arena football).*

75. *The Cleveland Crunch indoor soccer team.*

??

76. Who was the Elyria, Ohio, native who won the 1950 Heisman Trophy while playing tailback at Ohio State?

77. What Rocky River native called the Browns' radio play-by-play from 1985 to 1993?

78. Who seriously injured Indians catcher Ray Fosse's shoulder in a home plate collision at the 1970 All-Star Game?

79. Where were the Cleveland Browns Municipal Stadium offices located?

80. By what name was Polish-born Cleveland athlete Stanislawa Walasiewicz better known?

76. Vic Janowicz won the Heisman Trophy as a junior that year.

77. Nev Chandler.

78. Pete Rose.

79. Tower B.

80. Stella Walsh. She won the 100-yard dash for Poland in the 1932 Olympics and set 65 national and world track records by 1946. She was murdered during a 1980 robbery in Cleveland.

??

81. What sport was introduced to Cleveland Municipal Stadium in 1947?

82. What team did the Indians face in their first regular-season game against a National League opponent?

83. From 1946 to 1995, how many fans attended Browns regular-season home games at Municipal Stadium?
    a) 30 million
    b) 15 million
    c) 22 million
    d) 10 million

84. To what city did owner Nick Mileti move the WHA Cleveland Crusaders after the 1975–76 season?

85. Who was the only Cleveland Indians player selected for the 1963 All-Star Game played in Cleveland?

81. *Midget auto racing. A single 10-race event was to take place on a 40-foot-wide track on May 23, 1947. Only three races were held.*

82. *The St. Louis Cardinals, on June 14, 1997, at Busch Stadium in St. Louis. (The Tribe won, 8–3.)*

83. *c) just over 22 million. Attendance peaked at 621,000 in 1964.*

84. *Hollywood, Florida.*

85. *Pitcher Jim "Mudcat" Grant. He did not play in the game.*

? ?

86. What were the lower stands at the closed, west end of Municipal Stadium called during Browns games from the late-1980s to 1995?

87. In a girls' high-school softball game, the Royals are trying to top the Gators. Who is playing?

88. Yankee great Joe DiMaggio called him "the toughest I ever faced." What Indians pitcher was he talking about?

89. Name the *Plain Dealer* artist who caricatured Cleveland sports teams and their players from 1962 to 1992.

90. Name the pro basketball team that played in Cleveland from 1961 to 1962.

86. The "Junior Dawg Pound." At the far end of the field from the Dawg Pound, this section was reserved for "pups" and their families.

87. Regina High vs. Laurel School.

88. Mel Harder.

89. Dick Dugan.

90. The Cleveland Pipers, a member of the fledgling American Basketball League that folded at the end of 1962. Home games were played at Cleveland Public Hall.

???

91. What was the name of Cleveland's franchise in World Team Tennis?

92. Who was the youngest player for the Cleveland Indians?

93. Who scored the first touchdown in Cleveland Browns Stadium?

94. Which Cleveland-area club has hosted the most men's professional and amateur golf tournaments?

95. Whose bunt was misplayed by the Yankees in Game 2 of the 1998 American League championship series, allowing the Tribe to win and tie the series at one game apiece?

91. *The Cleveland Nets.*

92. *Bob Feller, who was 17 years old when he broke in with the team in 1936.*

93. *Leroy Hoard, running back for the Minnesota Vikings. On August 21, 1999, he scored on a six-yard run into the "Dawg Pound" end zone during the first quarter.*

94. *Canterbury Country Club, which has been the site of the Western Open (1932), the U.S. Open (1940 and 1946), the U.S. Amateur Championship (1964 and 1979), the PGA Championship (1973), the Senior Tournament Players Championship (1983–1986), and the U.S. Senior Open (1996).*

95. *Travis Fryman.*

96. Which two Cleveland-area high-schools have won the most state wrestling titles?

97. In 1969, Cleveland theatrical agent Syd Friedman organized the USA Daredevils, an all-woman team in what sport?

98. Who said "This isn't a ballpark. It's a cow pasture. A guy ought to have a horse to play the outfield"?

99. What was the name of the civic group formed in late 1995 to spearhead the effort to keep the Browns in Cleveland?

100. What Cleveland-area high-school basketball player scored 51 points in the 1979 state high-school championship game and went on to play for Ohio State and in the NBA?

96. *St. Edward (Lakewood) and Maple Heights.*

97. *Tackle football. The Daredevils were one of 12 such teams in Ohio.*

98. *Babe Ruth, remarking on Cleveland Municipal Stadium.*

99. *The Save Our Browns Committee.*

100. *Clark Kellogg, of St. Joseph High School (now Villa Angela-St. Joseph High School).*

101. Name the flamboyant Cleveland-born boxing promoter who rose to prominence in the 1970s promoting matches involving Muhammad Ali and later Mike Tyson.

102. What two Cleveland Indians players were the cover boys for *Sports Illustrated*'s 1987 preseason issue that advertised the Tribe as the team to beat (they lost 105 games that year)?

103. What Cleveland native and John Adams High grad played pro football with the Denver Broncos and later became an ESPN sports commentator?

104. Who won the PGA Tournament at Shaker Heights's Canterbury Country Club in 1973?

105. Who coined the nickname "Super Joe" for Indians slugger Joe Charboneau in 1980?

101. *Don King.*

102. *Outfielders Joe Carter and Cory Snyder.*

103. *Tom Jackson.*

104. *Jack Nicklaus.*

105. *Terry Pluto, sportswriter at the* Akron Beacon Journal.

106. What was the attendance capacity of Cleveland Municipal Stadium?

107. Gene Gibbons is the winningest high-school wrestling coach in Ohio, with a .700 record over 40 years (1960–1999). What school does he coach?

108. What was the capacity of League Park?

109. What Browns defensive lineman who played from 1984 to 1989 was affectionately known as "Big Daddy"?

110. Wayne Embry, former general manager of the Cleveland Cavaliers, had his college basketball number retired from which Ohio college?

106. *74,483.*

107. *Cleveland's John Marshall High School.*

108. *21,414.*

109. *Carl Hairston.*

110. *Miami University.*

111. What do Cleveland sports heroes Bernie Kosar of the Browns (1985–1993) and Bob Feller (1936–1956) of the Indians have in common?

112. What did Clevelander Charles Lupica do in 1949 in support of the Indians' second run at an American League pennant?

113. The first football game played at Cleveland Municipal Stadium in 1931 featured a Cleveland semi-pro team with a familiar name. What was it?

114. What famous personality was KO'd by Cleveland amateur boxer Happy Walsh, ending his brief amateur boxing career?

115. What Indians player from the early 1970s was known as the "Hawk"?

111. Both players wore the number 19.

112. He sat atop a 16-foot-tall flagpole from May 31 to September 25, 1949, when the Indians were eliminated from the pennant race.

113. The Cleveland Indians beat a semi-pro team from Pennsylvania, the Pennzoils, by a score of 10–0.

114. Leslie Townes Hope, a.k.a. Bob Hope, who fought under the name "Packy East" before giving up a career in the ring for one on the stage.

115. Ken Harrelson.

???

116. Who defeated the Browns in their last game of 1995?

117. What item of clothing was Cavaliers and Barons owner Nick Mileti's trademark in the 1970s?

118. Name the four Cleveland Indians who have won the American League Rookie of the Year award.

119. What former Browns offensive lineman, who made 194 consecutive starts for the team, served as the color commentator for Browns radio broadcasts?

120. The Cavs have had two players known simply by a letter of the alphabet. Which two letters, and who were the players?

116. *The expansion Jacksonville Jaguars beat the Browns on Christmas Eve, December 24, 1995, 24–21 in Jacksonville.*

117. *Mileti would meet and greet the crowds at the old Cleveland Arena wearing his famous full-length fur coat.*

118. *Herb Score (1955), Chris Chambliss (1972), Joe Charboneau (1980), and Sandy Alomar (1992).*

119. *Doug Dieken.*

120. *"Z," Zydrunas Ilgauskas, and "V," Vitaly Potapenko, who was traded to the Boston Celtics during the 1998–1999 season.*

???

121. What group headlined the first rock concert to be held at Cleveland Municipal Stadium?

122. What Cleveland Indian went by the nickname "Archie"?

123. Name the former Browns offensive left tackle who was elected to the Ohio State Senate.

124. What was placed on top of the lights at Cleveland's Municipal Stadium during the 1980s to help keep the pigeons away? A) sharpshooters; B) "Pigeons Keep Out" signs; C) wooden owls; D) spikes.

125. What was the score of the "Ten-Cent Beer Night" game between the Indians and the Texas Rangers at Municipal Stadium on June 4, 1974?

121. *The Beatles, on August 14, 1966, in front of more than 24,000 rowdy admirers. The Beatles performed on a stage that was built at second base, and a security fence surrounded the infield.*

122. *Outfielder Rick Manning (1975–1983), after the University of Mississippi and New Orleans Saints quarterback Archie Manning, who was well known at the time Rick was with the Indians.*

123. *Dick Schafrath, who played for the Browns from 1959 to 1971.*

124. *D) Wooden owls.*

125. *9–0, Texas. The umpires ordered a forfeit when, late in the game, rowdy Cleveland fans overloaded with cheap beer began jumping from the stands onto the field, threatening players. The score of a forfeit is always 9–0.*

? ?

126. What pro football team represented Cleveland in the American Football League in 1926?

127. For what do golfers have Clevelander Coburn Haskell to thank?

128. How many World Series victories did Bob Feller have in his career with the Indians?

129. Former Browns defensive end Al "Bubba" Baker no longer specializes in chasing QB's, but concentrates on another "Q" these days. What is it?

130. In what sport did the Cleveland Shamrocks compete?

126. *The Cleveland Panthers played for only one season in that league. The team started well, but was sued by creditors and disbanded, stranding players in Philadelphia. (In 1946, Paul Brown vetoed the name for Cleveland's team in the All America Football Conference so as not to associate it with financial failure.)*

127. *The rubber core inside a golf ball, which, in 1899, began giving golfers greater distance on their shots. Akron's B. F. Goodrich Company began manufacturing the new invention.*

128. *None. In 1948, "Rapid Robert" lost Games 1 and 5 to the Boston Braves; in 1954, against the New York Giants, he did not pitch.*

129. *He markets his own specialty "Bubba's Q" barbecue sauce.*

130. *Polo. The amateur team played their matches at the Cleveland Metroparks South Chagrin Reservation during the 1980s.*

? ?

131. Name the last Cleveland sports team to win a professional league championship.

132. What sports promotion did Indians owner Bill Veeck devise to bring female fans to Cleveland Stadium?

133. Browns quarterback Frank Ryan (1962–1968) held a Ph.D. in what academic field?

134. From 1972 to 1978, what sport could you play in the lower concourse of the Terminal Tower?

135. What was the largest crowd to watch a baseball game in Cleveland?

131. The Cleveland Crunch indoor soccer team won the NPSL 1998–1999 league championship title. (The Crunch were league champs for the 1995–1996 and 1993–1994 seasons, too.)

132. Ladies' Day. Veeck introduced the promotion in 1946; reduced ticket prices and giveaways like orchids and nylon stockings soon caught on in other major league cities.

133. Mathematics.

134. Tennis. Indoor courts were installed for the lunch-hour and after-work enjoyment of downtown workers.

135. At the national amateur baseball championship on October 15, 1915, more than 100,000 people gathered at Brookside Park to watch the Cleveland White Auto team defeat the Omaha Luxus team, 11–6.

CLEVELAND SPORTS TRIVIA QUIZ

? ?

136. What did noted *Cleveland Press* columnist Frank Gibbons describe with these words: "It's like the toppling of the Terminal Tower"?

137. Who built the Cleveland Arena in 1937 for Cleveland Barons games and other sporting events?

138. What Indians shortstop was the only player in major league history killed by a pitched ball?

139. NFL running back Robert Smith was a Buckeye at Ohio State and played high-school football as a Panther at what Cleveland-area high school?

140. Where did Danny Ferry play before joining the Cavaliers at the start of the 1990 season?

136. The 1963 firing of Browns coach Paul Brown.

137. Al Sutphin (at a cost of $1.5 million).

138. Ray Chapman, who was hit by a pitch thrown by Yankees pitcher Carl Mays in a game at the Polo Grounds in New York on August 16, 1920. He died within a day of the injury in a New York hospital and is buried in Lake View Cemetery.

139. Euclid High School.

140. He played for Il Messagerro of the Italian basketball league.

CLEVELAND SPORTS TRIVIA QUIZ Q ▶

? ?

141. Whom did Clevelander Joe Maxim defeat in 1952 for the light heavy-weight boxing title?

142. Name at least four of the 13 Cleveland Indians players from 1948 to the present who are enshrined in the Baseball Hall of Fame in Cooperstown, New York.

143. The Downtown Athletic Club of New York City annually awards a trophy to the best college football player in the country. For what Cleveland West Sider is it named?

144. A 16-year-old Chris Evert defeated England's Virginia Wade in what tennis event held in Cleveland in 1971?

145. Where were the Cleveland Indians Municipal Stadium offices located?

141. *Sugar Ray Robinson.*

142. *Bob Feller, pitcher, enshrined 1962; Lou Boudreau, shortstop and manager, 1970; Leroy "Satchel" Paige, pitcher, 1971; Early Wynn, pitcher, 1972; Ralph Kiner, out-fielder, 1975; Bob Lemon, pitcher, 1976; Al Lopez, catcher and manager, 1977; Frank Robinson, outfield and manager, 1982; Hoyt Wilhelm, pitch-er, 1985; Gaylord Perry, pitcher, 1991; Hal Newhouser, pitcher, 1992; Steve Carlton, pitcher, 1994; Phil Niekro, pitcher, 1997.*

143. *John Heisman, born on Cleveland's near West Side in 1869. Heisman was a foot-ball coach at Oberlin College, Buchtel College in Akron, and several universities in the South before becoming the director of the Downtown Athletic Club.*

144. *The Whitman Cup.*

145. *Tower A.*

? ?

146. Gib Shanley was the radio voice of the Cleveland Browns from 1961 to 1984. Who preceded him?

147. What is the nickname of the David N. Myers College (formerly Dyke College) basketball team?

148. On August 20, 1938, Indians reserve catcher Hank Helf stood at Public Square waiting for . . . what?

149. This 1991 Heisman Trophy winner from the University of Michigan played his high-school football at Cleveland's St. Joseph's High School. Name him.

150. What Cleveland Cavaliers player was known as the "Little General"?

146. *Bill McColgan, the primary broadcaster from 1954 to 1960.*

147. *The Demons.*

148. *A baseball thrown from the top of the Terminal Tower, 708 feet above street level.*

149. *Desmond Howard.*

150. *Bobby Washington (1970–1972).*

151. What 1991 movie used scenes filmed in Cleveland Municipal Stadium?

152. What do Indians pitchers Herb Score and 1997 rookie sensation Jaret Wright have in common?

153. Who has scored the most touchdowns for the Cleveland Browns?

154. What is the name of the Lumberjacks' mascot?

155. The Indians introduced what sartorial innovation on April 6,1929?

151. The Babe Ruth Story *used Cleveland Stadium because it most resembled ballparks of the Ruth era.*

152. *Indians uniform number 27.*

153. *Jim Brown, with 126 between 1957 and 1965.*

154. *Buzz the Beaver.*

155. *They placed numbers on the players' uniforms for the first time in professional baseball. It must have been good luck: Earl Averill, wearing number 5, hit the first pitch for a home run.*

? ?

156. More than a game, this high-school football match-up is a tradition. The Bulldogs vs. the Tigers. Who's playing?

157. Who was the Cleveland high-school hockey player drafted in the first round of the 1998 NHL draft?

158. Who hit the longest home run at Cleveland Municipal Stadium?

159. Who was the last Browns player to win the NFL's Most Valuable Player Award?

160. Who coached the Cleveland State University Vikings basketball team into the NCAA tournament in 1986?

156. Canton's McKinley High School and Massillon's Washington High School.

157. Michael Rupp of Brunswick and Lakewood's St. Edward High School was selected, as the ninth player overall, by the New York Islanders. (He was only the second Clevelander to be chosen in the pro hockey draft; the first was Todd Harkins, the forty-second player selected in 1988.)

158. Luke Easter, Indians first baseman, hit a 477-foot home run into the upper deck on June 23, 1950. Tribe radio announcer Jack Graney described Luke's prodigious home runs as "bazooka blasts."

159. Quarterback Brian Sipe in 1980 led Cleveland to its first playoff game since 1972 and completed 337 of 554 passes for 4,132 yards, 30 touchdowns, and 14 interceptions.

160. Kevin Mackey.

161. Lakewood High School and Eastlake North High School are both known as the . . . ?

162. Indians outfielder Leon Wagner (1964–1967) got this nickname from the slogan promoting his Los Angeles men's clothing store, "Get your rags from . . ."

163. All-pro defensive lineman Jerry Sherk almost died in 1979 . . . from what?

164. What is Cleveland's team in the outdoor United Systems of Independent Soccer Leagues?

165. What Cleveland Indians player shares the honor of hitting four consecutive home runs in a game with Lou Gehrig and Mike Schmidt?

161. *Rangers.*

162. *Daddy Wags.*

163. *A staph infection resulting from a leg injury.*

164. *The Cleveland Caps. (The "caps" represents the white-cap waves of Lake Erie.)*

165. *Rocky Colavito, who did it against the Baltimore Orioles at Memorial Stadium in Baltimore on June 10, 1959.*

??

166. What logo adorned the Cleveland Browns' football helmets when the team entered the NFL in 1950?

167. What is the official name of the brown, spicy mustard served with hot dogs since 1925 at League Park, Municipal Stadium, and Jacobs Field?

168. Name the Cleveland Indians outfielder who tied a major league record in 1998 for the most home runs (six) in three games.

169. What local college is the alma mater of former Miami Dolphins head coach and Pro Football Hall of Famer Don Shula?

170. "Every nineteen minutes, the place goes crazy." What place?

166. None. The Cleveland Browns helmet has never featured a logo.

167. Ballpark Mustard. (Although it is referred to as "stadium mustard" and "brown mustard," the official product name is Ballpark Mustard. It was introduced in 1925 by Joe Bertman Foods of Cleveland, Ohio.)

168. Manny Ramirez. On September 15, he slammed in three home runs against the Toronto Blue Jays. On the next two evenings at Jacobs Field, he greeted the Minnesota Twins with four more round-trippers.

169. John Carroll University.

170. Northfield Race Track.

??

171. Where does the Western Reserve Rowing Association row?

172. What local sporting "first" occurred on May 1, 1948?

173. What local Cleveland-area high-school football game would you be
    watching if you saw the Panthers play the Wildcats?

174. This legend from another sport entered the True Temper golf tournament
    at Acacia Country Club in 1937, in his only attempt at professional golf.
    Who was he?

175. What was Indians outfielder Albert Belle's home-run trot around the
    bases called?

171. *On the Cuyahoga River in the Flats.*

172. *The first live television broadcast of an Indians game from Cleveland Municipal Stadium.*

173. *Euclid High School vs. St. Ignatius or Mayfield High School.*

174. *George Herman "Babe" Ruth.*

175. *The "Albert Shuffle." In his trip around the bases, Albert would superstitiously stutter-step before touching each base.*

???

176. They're usually played in southern California, Florida, and Arizona, but one was played in Cleveland in 1947. What was it?

177. If you won the Thompson Trophy in 1929, in what event would you have competed?

178. Name two of the professional baseball teams that called Cleveland home before the Indians were named in 1915.

179. Name the Clevelander who was one of the University of Notre Dame's "Four Horsemen."

180. This Independence, Ohio, native played ten years with the NBA's Chicago Bulls. Who is he?

176. The Great Lakes Bowl, in which the University of Kentucky defeated Villanova 24–14.

177. The Cleveland Air Races.

178. The Forest Citys, the Spiders, the Blues, the Broncos, and the Naps.

179. Don Miller, originally from Defiance, Ohio, combined with Harry Stuhldreher, Elmer Layden, and Jim Crowley to form the famous backfield so named by sportswriter Grantland Rice in 1924. Stuhldreher was originally from Massillon, Ohio.

180. Tom Boerwinkle.

??

181. What do the world champion 1948 Cleveland Indians and the 1950 NFL champion Cleveland Browns have in common?

182. What New York Yankees player hit the line drive that struck Indians pitcher Herb Score in the eye on May 7, 1957?

183. What was the nickname of the 1980 Cleveland Browns?

184. Where is the Cleveland Nike Open golf tournament played?

185. What former Indians pitcher teamed with broadcaster Harry Jones to broadcast Indians TV games in 1973, 1974, and 1977?

181. *Both clubs won a special playoff game to advance to the championship game, the 1948 World Series and the 1950 NFL Championship, respectively. The Indians beat the Boston Red Sox 8–3; the Browns topped the New York Giants 8–3.*

182. *Gil McDougald.*

183. *The Kardiac Kids, because of their knack of winning in the final seconds.*

184. *Quail Hollow golf resort in Concord Township.*

185. *Jim "Mudcat" Grant.*

186. Name the Benedictine High School football coach who has the most victories of any Cleveland high-school coach.

187. What local sporting event includes cross-country running, swimming, fencing, pistol shooting, and equestrian jumping?

188. Which Browns fan has hit the most major league home runs?

189. How many regular-season NFL games did Cleveland Browns fullback Jim Brown miss during his nine-year career (1957–1965)?

190. Name the first Cleveland high-school basketball team to win a state basketball championship.

186. Augie Bossu.

187. The Great Lakes Pentathlon.

188. Henry Aaron, a self-avowed Browns fanatic since the 1950s, hit 755.

189. None.

190. East Technical High School (East Tech), which accomplished the feat in 1958.

??

191. Myron Scott is known as the father of what annual Akron event that takes place on a 953-foot downhill course?

192. When former Tribe pitcher Bob Lemon's number 21 was retired in the 1998 season, what current Indian had to give it up?

193. What St. Ignatius quarterback appeared as the character "B.D." in Gary Trudeau's *Doonesbury* cartoon?

194. From what small Midwestern city did the Lumberjacks move to Cleveland in 1992?

195. When the Indians moved to Jacob's Field, the Chief Wahoo sign was removed from atop the southeast corner of Municipal Stadium before that landmark was demolished. Where is it now?

191. *The All-American Soap Box Derby, held at Derby Downs racetrack.*

192. *Manager Mike Hargrove.*

193. *Brian Dowling, who was a classmate of Trudeau's at Yale University.*

194. *Muskegon, Michigan.*

195. *The Western Reserve Historical Society Museum, in University Circle.*

196. How many times has St. Ignatius football coach Chuck Kyle led the Wildcats to an Ohio High School State Football Championship?

197. This figure skater from Broadview Heights just missed qualifying for the 1998 Winter Olympics in Nagano, Japan, by placing fourth in the U.S. national figure-skating championship competition in January 1998. Name her.

198. Who said "I had total command, I could throw anything, anywhere I wanted" (1981)?

199. Name the Cleveland professional football team that won the 1924 NFL championship.

200. In what year did a Cleveland team first enter the NBA?

196. Seven: 1988, 1989, and 1991–1995.

197. Tonia Kwiatkowski.

198. Len Barker, after pitching a perfect game—no runs, no hits, no errors—on May 15, 1981, against the Toronto Blue Jays.

199. The Cleveland Bulldogs, who had been the Canton Bulldogs prior to 1924. The team disbanded after the 1925 season.

200. 1946, when the Cleveland Rebels were the town's entry in the NBA's inaugural season.

??

201. Where was the Cleveland area's first golf club located?

202. Who threw out the first pitch before the first regular-season game in Jacobs Field?

203. When he played for the Browns from 1986 to 1991, his California license plate read "Webstar." Who is he?

204. Name the professional hockey teams that have played in Cleveland.

205. What Indians outfielder (1908–1922) went straight to the radio booth in 1923 and called Indians games until 1954?

201. *In Bratenahl. Cleveland industrialist Samuel Mather organized the Cleveland Golf Club in 1895.*

202. *Left-hander William Jefferson Clinton.*

203. *Wide receiver Webster Slaughter.*

204. *The Indians (1929–1934) and the Falcons (1934–1937) of the International Hockey League; the Barons (1937–1973) of the American Hockey League; the Crusaders (1972–1976) of the World Hockey Association; the Barons (1976–1978) of the National Hockey League; and the Lumberjacks (1992–present) of the International Hockey League.*

205. *Jack Graney, who was the first professional athlete to start a second career as a broadcaster.*

? ?

206. Who was the Cleveland Barons player and coach who led them to Cleveland's last professional hockey championship in 1964?

207. What was the name of Clevelander Robert Manry's 13 ½ foot sailboat, in which he crossed the Atlantic Ocean in 1965?

208. Who were the two Cleveland Indians pitchers killed in a boating accident during 1992 spring training in Florida?

209. Whom did the Browns play in their first National League football game in 1950?

210. Besides the well-known Bill Fitch, Lenny Wilkens, and Mike Fratello, the Cavaliers have had eight other head coaches since 1970. Name at least three.

206. Fred Glover.

207. Tinkerbelle. *At that time, it was the smallest craft to make the Atlantic crossing.*

208. Steve Olin and Tim Crews.

209. The Philadelphia Eagles. *The upstart Browns, winners of four AAFC championships from 1946 to 1949, beat the defending NFL champs 35–10 on September 16, 1950.*

210. Stan Albeck, Bill Musselman (twice), Don Delaney, Chuck Daley, Bob Kloppenburg, Tom Nissalke, George Karl, Gene Littles.

??

211. What did the *Plain Dealer* call the bowling contest it sponsored in the 1960s and '70s?

212. Which former Indians slugger titled his autobiography *Triumph Born of Tragedy*?

213. Browns running back Jim Brown (1957–1965) was an All-American in what two sports at Syracuse University?

214. When the Tigers face the Red Raiders in football, basketball, or baseball, what rival high schools are playing?

215. What Wooster native pitched a no-hitter against the Indians in 1967 for the Minnesota Twins (and eventually earned induction into the Baseball Hall of Fame)?

211. *"I Beat the Champ."* Area bowlers compared their scores to those of professional championship bowlers.

212. *Andre Thornton.*

213. *Football and lacrosse.*

214. *Cleveland Heights and Shaker Heights.*

215. *Dean Chance.*

216. What is the caricature of Art Modell doing on the cover of *Sports Illustrated*'s December 5, 1995, issue?

217. The Cleveland Crusaders hockey team played their first game at the Richfield Coliseum on October 27, 1974. What was the result?

218. After he hit his 100th career home run, what did Cleveland outfielder Jimmy Piersall do?

219. The Browns played 56 games in the All America Football Conference from 1946 to 1949. How many did they lose?

220. Who was the Cleveland Cavaliers' first college draft pick in 1970?

216. He is sucker-punching a Browns "Dawg" character, which symbolized his treatment of Cleveland football fans when he announced the Browns' move to Baltimore.

217. Disappointed fans. The game was postponed due to melting ice. The second home opener on October 30th could not be played either for the same reason.

218. He circled the bases backwards.

219. Four. The Browns reigned as AAFC champs every year and finished their AAFC tenure with a record of 47 wins, 4 losses, and 3 ties.

220. John Johnson, from the University of Iowa.

? ?

221. Who hosted *Sportsline* on several local radio stations from 1966 to 1988?

222. Indians pitcher Phil Niekro (1986–1987) was nicknamed after the pitch that was his specialty. Name the pitch and his nickname.

223. What team was the Cleveland Browns' first regular-season opponent in their professional debut in the All America Football Conference in 1946?

224. What public relations disaster did Cleveland Competitors team owner Ted Stepien stage in August 1980?

225. Who was the first radio broadcaster for the Cleveland Indians?

221. The Fabulous Peter J. "Pete" Franklin.

222. Phil threw a knuckleball and earned the name "Knucksie."

223. The Miami Seahawks.

224. A softball toss from the top of the Terminal Tower. One ball damaged a car and another injured a spectator standing near Public Square.

225. Thomas "Red" Manning called the first Indians game on radio station WTAM in 1928. (After undergoing several call-letter changes over the years, WTAM radio again carries Tribe games today.)

???

226. What is the real name of "Big Dawg"?

227. What Indians announcer was the pitchman for a local aluminum siding company whose phone number was "Garfield 1-2323"?

228. Name the Indians broadcaster who played for the New York Yankees, Seattle Pilots, Milwaukee Brewers, and Oakland Athletics.

229. Who was "the man in the brown suit"?

230. Name the Canton resident who won Olympic gold in 1972 for the 800-meter event (wearing his trademark golf hat).

226. *John Thompson.*

227. *Jimmy Dudley. (Dudley was inducted into the Baseball Hall of Fame's section for broadcasters in 1997.)*

228. *Mike Hegan.*

229. *Abe Abraham, who caught extra points and field goals at the closed end of the Stadium during Browns games from the late 1940s to the early 1970s.*

230. *Dave Wottle.*

???

231. What local country club was home to the World Series of Golf?

232. Who was the highest-paid Indians player, based on annual salary, at the end of the 1998 season?

233. Who said "The gleam, men, remember the gleam"?

234. From 1979 to 1988, Cleveland real estate developer Bart Wolstein owned a professional sports franchise in which sport?

235. Two Indians radio broadcasters teamed up for eight years (1957–61; 1962–64) of first-rate play-by-play, but they detested each other outside the radio booth. Who were they?

231. Firestone Country Club.

232. Kenny Lofton, at $7.55 million annually.

233. Marty Schottenheimer, Browns head coach, during the 1986 season. He was referring to the reflection of light off the silver Super Bowl trophy.

234. Indoor soccer (the Cleveland Force).

235. Jimmy Dudley and Bob Neal.

? ?

236. Who threw the longest pass in the history of the Cleveland Browns? Who caught it?

237. What well-known golf-course architect designed both the Blue and White courses at Fowler's Mill Golf Club in Chesterland, Ohio?

238. What Indians outfielder was a basketball standout at the University of Arizona?

239. The Hilltoppers are facing the Comets in a Friday-night football contest. What two schools are playing?

240. What Cleveland Cavaliers uniform numbers have been retired, and who wore them?

236. *Bernie Kosar threw a 97-yard touchdown pass to wide receiver Webster Slaughter on October 23, 1989, in a Monday Night Football game against the Chicago Bears.*

237. *Pete Dye.*

238. *Kenny Lofton.*

239. *Chardon High School (Hilltoppers) and Solon (Comets).*

240. *7—Bobby "Bingo" Smith; 22—Larry Nance; 34—Austin Carr; 42—Nate Thurmond.*

???

241. Where were Cleveland's amateur boxing Golden Gloves matches held during the 1960s and 1970s?

242. Where do the Indians conduct spring training?

243. What 1983 Browns second-round draft choice chose the 1984 Olympics instead of signing with the team?

244. Who won the United States Senior Open golf tournament at Canterbury Country Club in 1996?

245. In 1970, what Canton-born former Kent State University catcher was named American League Rookie of the Year as a member of the New York Yankees?

241. *Navy Park gymnasium at Ridge and Clinton Roads.*

242. *Chain O' Lakes Park in Winter Haven, Florida.*

243. *Ron Brown, who was a wide receiver and sprinter at Arizona State.*

244. *Dave Stockton.*

245. *Thurman Munson. Canton's minor league stadium is named Thurman Munson Stadium.*

246. "Bam-Bam," the nickname for hard-hitting Browns linebacker Dick Ambrose (1975–1983), came from a character on what TV show?

247. What City of Cleveland public golf course features a "Red" and a "Blue" course?

248. Name the Atlanta Braves player whose home run in Game 6 of the 1995 World Series won the championship for the Braves.

249. What Browns offensive tackle (1988–1995) was known as "T-Bone"?

250. The Cleveland Cavaliers set what NBA record against the Miami Heat on December 17, 1991?

246. The Flintstones.

247. Highland Park Golf Course.

248. David Justice.

249. Tony Jones.

250. Largest margin of victory, 148–80.

??

251. The Richfield Coliseum was affectionately referred to as what??

252. Who tore knee ligaments during the fourth game of the 1995 American League championship series against Seattle at Jacobs Field and spent the rest of the series on crutches?

253. Who said "You can accomplish anything you want, as long as you don't care who gets the credit"?

254. Akron native Phil Boggs won world titles three times (1973, 1975, and 1978) in what sport?

255. Which Indians outfielder hurled three scoreless innings of relief in 1958?

251. *The Big House on the Prairie.*

252. *Slider, the mascot. He fell off the right field wall.*

253. *Blanton Collier, Browns coach from 1963 to 1970.*

254. *Springboard diving.*

255. *Rocky Colavito, against the Detroit Tigers on August 13, 1958.*

256. What team did Brian Sipe leave the Browns for after the 1983 season?

257. What *Akron Beacon Journal* sportswriter has written more than 15 sports books and has been named Ohio Sportswriter of the Year four times?

258. What Indians pitcher from the 1920s pitched seven innings without a called ball?

259. Name the Kent State University and professional football player who earned the nickname "The Human Bowling Ball."

260. Name the first black professional basketball head coach.

256. *The New Jersey Generals of the USFL.*

257. *Terry Pluto.*

258. *Stan Coveleski.*

259. *Don Nottingham.*

260. *John McClendon, coach of the Cleveland Pipers of the American Basketball League in 1961 and 1962.*

???

261. How many hockey seasons did the Crusaders play in Cleveland?

262. What Indians outfielder was the subject of the book *Fear Strikes Out*?

263. Cleveland's South High School and Holy Name High School football teams played for a symbolic trophy during the 1950s and 1960s. What was it called?

264. Where was the first Grand Prix of Cleveland auto race held?

265. What Collinwood native and Cleveland State University graduate played shortstop for the Cleveland Indians from 1980 to 1982?

261. Four.

262. Jimmy Piersall.

263. The "Pig Iron" trophy. The schools battled for a slab of pig iron mounted on a board, symbolizing the jobs that grandparents and great-grandparents of the players had held in Cleveland steel mills.

264. At Burke Lakefront Airport.

265. Jerry Dybzinski, nicknamed the "Dibber."

??

266. What was the halftime score of the Cleveland Browns–Baltimore Colts 1964 NFL championship game played at Municipal Stadium?

267. How many pairs of brothers have played pro ball in Cleveland—one as an Indian, one as a Brown? Name them.

268. Who holds the single-season home run record for the Cleveland Indians: Albert Belle or Rocky Colavito?

269. In the famous double-overtime victory over the New York Jets in the 1986 season playoffs, which Browns player finally kicked the game-winning field goal after missing one earlier?

270. With five seconds left in the game, this Cavalier dropped a bank shot to win Game 7 of the 1976 first-round playoffs against the Washington Bullets. Who is he?

266. *Incredibly, neither team had scored by halftime, a big boost for the Browns, who were pregame underdogs. Final score: Browns 27, Colts 0.*

267. *Four: Leroy Kelly (Browns) and Pat Kelly (Indians); Ron Johnson (Browns) and Alex Johnson (Indians); Mike Pagel (Browns) and Karl Pagel (Indians); Wayne Kirby (Indians) and Terry Kirby (Browns).*

268. *Albert Belle, with 50 home runs in 1995. (Colavito is tied for third place with 42.)*

269. *Mark Moseley.*

270. *Dick Snyder.*

??

271. What Cleveland-based cosmetic company first sponsored a 10K run for women in 1976?

272. In 1959, what football player did Indians general manager Frank Lane try to sign to a baseball contract?

273. Tom Tupa of Brecksville and Ohio State University is in the NFL record books for being the first player to do what?

274. What popular Lake Erie sporting fish goes by the scientific name *Stizostedion vitreum*?

275. What Indians pitcher was given the nickname "Sudden"?

271. *Bonne Belle Inc. of Lakewood, Ohio, initiated this exclusive women's run in Cleveland, New York, Boston, Aspen, and Atlanta.*

272. *Jim Brown. He rejected the offer and got an $8,000 a year raise from the Browns.*

273. *Score a two-point conversion—in the first game of the 1994 season, after the league rule change. His nickname ever since has been "Two Point Tupa."*

274. *The walleye.*

275. *Sam McDowell (1961–1971). An umpire tagged him with this name because his pitches were so fast that "all of a sudden" they reached the plate.*

276. What is located at 76 Lou Groza Boulevard?

277. Outstanding sports figures who are born and reared in Cleveland, bring recognition to the city through sporting accomplishments, and who continue to reside in the city, are eligible for what honor?

278. How many times has major league baseball's All-Star Game been played in Cleveland?

279. What are the most points scored by the Browns in a single game?

280. Cleveland Cavaliers guard Lloyd Free (1982–1986) was known by what other name?

276. *The Cleveland Browns training facility and administrative offices. The street name was changed by the city of Berea in 1998 to honor the longtime Berea resident and Browns Hall of Famer.*

277. *Membership in the Greater Cleveland Sports Hall of Fame (organized in 1976).*

278. *Five. Cleveland has hosted the midsummer classic in 1935, 1954, 1963, 1981, and 1997.*

279. *Sixty-two. They did it twice: on December 6, 1953, they beat the New York Giants 62–14; on November 7, 1954, they defeated the Washington Redskins 62–3.*

280. *World B. Free. (He averaged 23 points per game for the Cavs during his stint in Cleveland.)*

281. At various times, this Cleveland native and John Adams High School grad owned the Indians, Cavaliers, Barons, and Crusaders. Name him.

282. Name the two Cleveland Indians who appeared on the Wheaties cereal box after the team's appearance in the 1995 World Series?

283. What number did Jim Brown wear in his first game with the Browns, a preseason exhibition game in 1957?

284. The city of Cleveland owns and operates which two public golf courses?

285. What Indians pitcher played defensive back for Cornell University in 1985 before transferring to the University of Connecticut?

281. *Nick Mileti.*

282. *Kenny Lofton and Jose Mesa.*

283. *Number 45. He changed to number 32 for the next game and wore it every other game of his career.*

284. *Seneca Golf Course in Broadview Heights and Highland Park Golf Course in Highland Hills. Both courses are thirty-six-hole layouts.*

285. *Charles Nagy (he played football on Cornell's freshman team).*

???

286. What Cleveland-area high school did Miami Dolphins receiver O. J. McDuffie attend?

287. What Cleveland attorney pioneered the representation and promotion of professional athletes and helped found the International Management Group (IMG)?

288. This Indians pitcher ranks first in game appearances (582), second in career wins (223), and fifth in team career strikeouts (1,161), was named to the American League All-Star team four times, but is not enshrined in the Hall of Fame at Cooperstown. Who is he?

289. Name the first coach of the National Professional Soccer League's Cleveland Crunch indoor soccer team.

290. Who was covering the Chicago Bulls' Michael Jordan during the 1989 NBA playoffs when he beat the Cavaliers in the final seconds, with "the shot"?

286. *Hawken School.*

287. *Mark McCormack.*

288. *Mel Harder. His career spanned twenty seasons, 1928–1947, the most by any Indian.*

289. *Kai Haaskivi, the popular former Cleveland Force soccer player.*

290. *Craig Ehlo.*

291. Who is known as Cleveland's "Mr. Tennis" for his work in promoting amateur and professional tennis during the 1960s, '70s, and '80s?

292. Who was the oldest player to play for the Cleveland Indians?

293. He played linebacker for the Buffalo Bills in the 1960s, played in two American Football League championship games, and later coached the Cleveland Browns. Who is he?

294. What Cleveland suburb is New York Yankees owner George Steinbrenner's hometown?

295. What milestone did Babe Ruth reach at League Park in 1929?

291. *Bob Malaga.*

292. *Phil Niekro was 48 years old when he pitched for the Tribe in the 1987 season.*

293. *Marty Schottenheimer, Browns head coach, 1984–1989.*

294. *Bay Village.*

295. *The Babe hit his 500th career home run.*

??

296. Which Browns player was released because management determined he suffered from "diminishing physical skills"?

297. Who won the first Budweiser-Cleveland 500 Grand Prix auto race in 1982?

298. Indians right-hander Wynn Hawkins is probably best known for giving up whose 500th home run in 1960?

299. What was the name of the weekly Cleveland Browns highlight show hosted by Ken Coleman during the 1960s?

300. What national basketball powerhouse did the CSU Vikings basketball team defeat in the first round of the 1986 NCAA Tournament?

296. *Quarterback Bernie Kosar, in 1993.*

297. *Bobby Rahal.*

298. *Ted Williams.*

299. *The Quarterback Club.*

300. *The Indiana Hoosiers, coached by Bobby Knight.*

???

301. Local anglers have dubbed Lake Erie the "_____ capital of the world."

302. Who did the Indians receive from the Detroit Tigers in the infamous Rocky Colavito trade of April 17, 1960?

303. Browns linebacker Tom Cousineau attended what Cleveland-area high school?

304. What entertainer gave the only concert ever held in Jacobs Field?

305. How did Indians player Carlos Martinez manage to score an unusual home run against the Texas Rangers on May 26, 1993?

301. *Walleye.*

302. *Outfielder Harvey Kuenn.*

303. *St. Edward High School in Lakewood, Ohio.*

304. *Jimmy Buffet.*

305. *The ball he hit bounced off the head of outfielder Jose Canseco and went over the fence.*

? ?

306. In 1941, Irma Beede of Youngstown, Ohio, earned the nickname, "the Betsy Ross of professional football." Why?

307. What do the initials C.Y.C. stand for?

308. Which Indians president concocted a plan to permanently close the outfield bleachers in 1985?

309. What West Side bowling landmark closed in 1999 after 43 years of operation?

310. The Cavaliers' 1982 first- and second-round draft picks had last names that rhymed. Who were they?

306. *She sewed the first modern-day penalty flag for use by referees in a game. Her husband, Youngstown State coach Dick Beede, gave the flag to an official on October 16, 1941, thinking it would be less distracting than a horn or a whistle.*

307. *The Cleveland Yacht Club. (The club was originally organized in 1878 as the Cleveland Yachting Association but moved from downtown Cleveland to its current home at the mouth of the Rocky River in 1914.)*

308. *Peter Bavasi. The plan was met with angry fan reaction, and Bavasi kept them open for day games.*

309. *Hornack Bowling Center in Lakewood.*

310. *John Bagley and Dave Magley.*

311. Name the 1966 movie starring Jack Lemmon and Walter Matthau that included footage of the Cleveland Browns, Municipal Stadium, and Cleveland fans.

312. Name the three Cleveland Indians in the top 100 baseball players of all time, according to the *Sporting News* 1998 analysis. (Hint: All three are pitchers.)

313. Six Cleveland Browns players won the college Heisman Trophy. Name them.

314. In 1929, Cleveland acquired its first pro hockey team. What was its name?

315. Who holds the record for the longest home run in Jacobs Field?

311. The Fortune Cookie.

312. Sporting News *ranked Satchel Paige at 19, Bob Feller at 36, and Early Wynn at 100. Who is ranked No.1? Babe Ruth, of course.*

313. *Les Horvath, 1944; Howard "Hopalong" Cassady, 1955; Ernie Davis, 1961; Charles White, 1979; Vinny Testaverde, 1986; Ty Detmer, 1990.*

314. *The Indians.*

315. *Mark McGwire, who was playing for the Oakland A's when his 485-foot blast on April 30, 1997, hit the scoreboard's Budweiser beer advertisement. Orel Hershiser served up the pitch.*

???

316. What Benedictine High grad played for the Browns from 1953 to 1959 and became an NFL head coach with four Super Bowl victories?

317. Where did most of Cleveland Municipal Stadium end up in 1997?

318. Who has been beating his drum in the bleachers at Tribe games since 1973?

319. Name the two Browns running backs who ran for more than 1,000 yards each in a single season.

320. Who was the Cavaliers' wacky center/forward found waiting in a concession-stand line while his team's first NBA game got under way in Buffalo in 1970?

316. *Chuck Noll.*

317. *In Lake Erie. (Sections of the brick and concrete were dumped in the lake to form a fishing reef.)*

318. *John Adams.*

319. *Kevin Mack (1,104 yards) and Earnest Byner (1,002 yards) did it in 1985.*

320. *Gary Suiter, who was notorious for driving coach Bill Fitch crazy.*

??

321. What former Boston Bruin all-star played goalie for the World Hockey Association Cleveland Crusaders?

322. What was the name of the 1949 movie about a troubled youth who befriended the 1948 Cleveland Indians baseball team?

323. Because of his unusual quickness for a big man, Browns defensive tackle Walter Johnson (1965–1976) carried what nickname?

324. Who was Hal, of "Ask Hal, the Referee"?

325. How old was Leroy "Satchel" Paige when he joined the Indians in 1948?

321. *Gerry Cheevers.*

322. The Kid from Cleveland.

323. *"Zoom."*

324. *Hal Lebovitz answered readers' questions about sports rules or sports in general in this* Plain Dealer *column during the 1960s, '70s, and '80s. He went on to write for the* Lake County News Herald *and the* Lorain Morning Journal.

325. *Forty-two—officially, though his real age was never conclusively established.*

???

326. What was the high-school football championship game between Cleveland's West and East Senate conferences called?

327. What Akron resident founded the Professional Bowling Association (PBA)?

328. What was the nickname of the Indians' flash-in-the-pan rookie Harold Hodge, who went four-for-four to start the 1971 season?

329. John Carroll University quarterback Larry Wanke received what "honor" in 1991?

330. What two Cleveland-area high schools' girls' teams have won three con-secutive state high-school track titles?

326. The Charity Game. It originated in 1931, with proceeds going to Cleveland-area charities. The last Charity Game was played at the Stadium in 1970.

327. Eddy Elias.

328. Gomer, because his speech reminded teammates of Jim Nabors' "Gomer Pyle" character.

329. He was picked as the last player in the 1991 NFL college draft. As the NFL's "Mr. Irrelevant" (the title granted each year to the very last player taken in the draft), Wanke was showered with a variety of gifts, including a trip to Disney World.

330. Collinwood High School (Division I, 1997–1999) and Beaumont High School (Division II, 1997–1999.) Beaumont also won the Division I crown in 1996, which really gives them four straight track titles.

???

331. At the college level, John Carroll University sports teams are the Blue Streaks. What local girls' high-school teams go by the same name?

332. Indians home League Park went by what other name from 1920 to 1927?

333. The annual football game between Lakewood's St. Edward and St. Ignatius has become known by what nickname?

334. What was the largest crowd to watch a sporting event at Cleveland Municipal Stadium (1932–1995)?

335. Who was the last Indians player to hit for the cycle (a single, double, triple, and a homer in one game)?

331. *Magnificat High School in Rocky River.*

332. *Dunn Field, after the team's owner, James Dunn. (After Dunn's death in 1927, the park was again named League Park.)*

333. *The "Holy War."*

334. *Game 5 of the 1948 World Series, the Indians against the Boston Braves—86,288. (The Browns' first Monday Night Football game is second, with 85,703 fans on September 21, 1970.)*

335. *Andre Thornton, on April 22, 1978, against the Boston Red Sox.*

???

336. What is Bernie Kosar's hometown?

337. Mike Durbin of Chagrin Falls has won a record three Firestone Tournament of Champions titles—in what sport?

338. Indians pitchers Mike Kekich (1973) and Fritz Peterson (1974–1975) were infamous for what unusual behavior in 1973, when both pitched for the New York Yankees before being traded to Cleveland?

339. Who said "I am good for Cleveland . . . I think you're all lucky that I'm here"? (1984)

340. Name the Cavaliers' starting line-up for their first game in 1970.

336. Boardman, Ohio.

337. Professional bowling.

338. The two swapped not only wives but entire families—and houses. Kekich's union with Peterson's wife didn't last; Peterson and Kekich's wife remained married.

339. Sam Rutigliano, Browns head coach, two weeks before he was fired.

340. McCoy McLemore, Bingo Smith, Luther Rackley, Johnny Egan, and John Warren.

? ?

341. What Cleveland Cavaliers and Cleveland Browns players were high-school classmates and teammates in Akron, Ohio?

342. What Indians infielder is the only major leaguer to hit home runs from both sides of the plate in the same inning?

343. Which two Cleveland Browns players are credited with naming the bleacher at Cleveland Municipal Stadium the "Dawg Pound"?

344. Name the pair of Akron figure-skaters who each won Olympic gold medals.

345. Match the home run description with the Cleveland sportscaster:
    1. "That ball's going, going . . . gone!"   a. Jack Corrigan
    2. "Way back . . . waaay back . . . gone!"   b. Jimmy Dudley
    3. "It's touch-'em-all time!"   c. Tom Hamilton

341. *Frank Stams (Browns, 1992–1994) and Jerome Lane (Cavaliers, 1992–1993).*

342. *Carlos Baerga, in the seventh inning of a game against the Yankees on April 8, 1993.*

343. *Hanford Dixon and Frank Minniefield.*

344. *Hayes Jenkins (1956) and Carol Heiss (1960).*

345. *1 (b), 2 (c), 3 (a).*

346. Which running back, drafted by the Browns in 1962 to team with Jim Brown, never played a single down and died of leukemia in 1963?

347. Name the first sporting event held at Cleveland Municipal Stadium.

348. What Indians baseball executive labeled the city a "sleeping giant," referring to the potential of the fans to support a winning sports team?

349. Name the three Ohio State football players selected by the Cleveland Browns in the first round of the NFL college draft.

350. How many games did the Cleveland Cavaliers win in their NBA season in 1970?

346. *Ernie Davis.*

347. *A world heavyweight championship fight between Max Schmelling and Young Striblingon, on July 31, 1931, before a crowd of 36,936.*

348. *Gabe Paul, who served stints as team president and general manager in the 1960s and '70s.*

349. *Defensive lineman Jim Houston (1960), wide receiver Paul Warfield (1964), and linebacker Craig Powell (1995).*

350. *Sixteen. They lost 67.*

351. What two "sins" were taxed in Cuyahoga County to help fund Jacobs Field and Gund Arena?

352. In 1948, what were the Cleveland Indians fans who populated the bleacher section of Municipal Stadium called?

353. What nationally televised sports event was inaugurated in Cleveland on September 21, 1970?

354. What was the last sporting event held at the Richfield Coliseum?

355. What was Mike Hargrove's nickname when he played for the Indians from 1979 to 1985?

351. *Alcohol and tobacco.*

352. *"Bleacher Bugs." The Cleveland Press published the name in an article, and it caught on.*

353. *ABC's Monday Night Football. The Browns beat the New York Jets by a score of 31–21 at Cleveland Municipal Stadium.*

354. *An exhibition minor league Cleveland Lumberjacks hockey game on September, 1994.*

355. *"The Human Rain Delay," because he took so much time adjusting his cap, batting gloves, and uniform before every pitch.*

356. What local television sports anchor burned a miniature Iranian flag at the conclusion of one of his evening sports report during the 1979–1980 Iranian hostage crisis?

357. On what local golf course was a player shot to death on the 16th tee in an alleged gang slaying?

358. What Cleveland Indian was known as the "Bogalusa Bomber"?

359. What is the name of Massillon's Washington High School football stadium?

360. What 1985 Cavaliers rookie was nicknamed "Dinner Bell"?

356. Gib Shanley.

357. Orchard Hills in Chesterland.

358. Slugging outfielder Charley Spikes (1973–1977), after his hometown of Bogalusa, Louisiana.

359. Paul Brown Stadium, in honor of the former Massillon coach and first coach of the Cleveland Browns.

360. "Dinner Bell" Mel Turpin, who earned this name with his appetite.

???

361. Who is known as the "Father of Yachting" in Northeast Ohio?

362. Fifteen perfect games have been pitched in major league baseball history. How many have Cleveland teams participated in?

363. What Cuyahoga Falls native intercepted a pass for a TD in Super Bowl XVIII, helping the Los Angeles Raiders win the NFL Championship in 1984?

364. Cleveland "power couple" Howard Prechtel and Noi Phumchaona have won 11 consecutive world championships in what sport?

365. What Brush High School (Lyndhurst) grad won the American League's Cy Young Award in 1980?

361. *George Gardner organized yachting as a sports activity in 1878 when he founded the Cleveland Yachting Association.*

362. *Three. Twice as winners: on May 15, 1981, Len Barker threw a perfect game against the Toronto Blue Jays, and on October 2, 1908, Addie Joss was perfect against the Chicago White Sox. Way back in 1880, Cleveland was the victim of a perfect game thrown by John Richmond of the Worcester, Massachusetts, team.*

363. *Jack Squirek.*

364. *Weightlifting. This husband-and-wife team has ruled the International Weightlifting Association's world championships from 1988 to 1998. (At 115 pounds, Noi Phumchaona was recognized as the best female lifter at the 1998 IWA meet.)*

365. *Steve Stone.*

366. Name the Cleveland Browns player who switched his last name and uniform number for the opening game of the 1993 season.

367. It's the Redmen vs. the Green Wave on the hardwood in a local high-school basketball contest. Who's playing?

368. What NBC sports personality was the unlucky recipient of a verbal tirade by the Indians' Albert Belle concerning her pregame presence in the dugout during the 1995 World Series?

369. What was the name of the infamous play that ended the Browns' "Kardiac Kids" season in the 1980 playoffs against the Oakland Raiders at Municipal Stadium?

370. What Cavaliers player was the first to record a "triple-double" (points, rebounds, and assists are in double figures for a game)?

366. *Wide receiver Michael Jackson changed his last name to Dyson and his number from "1" to "81" for the home opener against Cincinnati. The name change honored his father; the number change was due to an NFL rule.*

367. *Parma vs. Holy Name.*

368. *Hannah Storm.*

369. *"Red Right 88." Brian Sipe's pass intended for Ozzie Newsome was intercepted in the end zone by Oakland's Mike Davis.*

370. *Clarence "Foots" Walker, against the Atlanta Hawks in 1979.*

??

371. Match the Cleveland area/Northern Ohio college with its nickname:

1. Cleveland State University	a. Zips
2. Case Western Reserve University	b. Fighting Scots
3. John Carroll University	c. Yeomen
4. Baldwin-Wallace College	d. Vikings
5. Kent State University	e. Spartans
6. Hiram College	f. Blue Streaks
7. Mount Union College	g. Yellow Jackets
8. Oberlin College	h. Golden Flashes
9. Wooster College	i. Terriers
10. Akron University	j. Purple Raiders

372. Who was the last Cleveland Indian to win the American League batting title?

373. How many head coaches did the Browns have between 1946 and 1995? Name them.

371. 1 (d), 2 (e), 3 (f), 4 (g), 5 (h), 6 (i), 7 (j), 8 (c), 9 (b), 10 (a).

372. Bobby Avila, who batted .341 for the 1954 season.

*373. Paul Brown, 1946–1962; Blanton Collier, 1963–1970; Nick Skorich, 1971–1974;
Forrest Gregg, 1975–1977; Dick Modzelewski, 1977 (1 game);
Sam Rutigliano, 1978–1984; Marty Schottenheimer, 1984–1988; Bud Carson,
1989–1990; Jim Shofner, 1990 (8 games); Bill Belichick, 1991–1995.*

? ?

374. Match the athlete with the Cleveland sports team:

1. Peaches Bartkowicz	a. Cleveland Crunch
2. Bob Waterfield	b. Cleveland Indians
3. Larry Siegfried	c. St. Ignatius High School
4. Bob Whidden	d. Cleveland Nets
5. Ali Kazemaini	e. Cleveland Crusaders
6. Pepe Pearson	f. Cleveland Pipers
7. Willie Kirkland	g. Cleveland Cavaliers
8. Joe Pickens	h. Cleveland Browns
9. Walt Frazier	i. Euclid High School
10. Tommy Williams	j. Cleveland Force
11. Craig Powell	k. Cleveland Rams
12. Otto Orf	l. Cleveland Barons

375. How many members of the Cleveland Browns are enshrined in the Pro Football Hall of Fame in Canton, Ohio? Name them.

374. 1 (d), 2 (k), 3 (f), 4 (e), 5 (j), 6 (i), 7 (b), 8 (c), 9 (g), 10 (l), 11 (h), 12. (a).

375. Fourteen: Otto Graham, quarterback (1946–1955), inducted 1965; Dante Lavelli, wide receiver (1946–1956), inducted 1975; Paul Brown, head coach (1946–1962), inducted 1967; Marion Motley, running back (1946–1953), inducted 1968; Jim Brown, running back (1957–1965), inducted 1971; Len Ford, defensive line (1950–1957), inducted 1976; Lou Groza, offensive lineman and kicker (1946–1967), inducted 1974; Frank Gatski, offensive line (1946–1953), inducted 1985; Bill Willis, offensive line (1946–1953), inducted 1977; Paul Warfield, wide receiver (1958–1961), inducted 1983; Bobby Mitchell, running back (1958–1961), inducted 1983; Mike McCormack, offensive line (1954–1962), inducted 1984; Leroy Kelly, running back (1964–1973), inducted 1994; Ozzie Newsome, tight end (1978–1990), inducted 1999.

???

376. Who made the first Indians regular-season hit at the new Jacobs field?

377. Name the welterweight boxer who died as a result of his title fight with Sugar Ray Robinson at the Cleveland Arena on July 2, 1947.

378. What all-star NBA player was drafted out of Ohio State by the Cleveland Browns in 1961?

379. Indians hitting coach Charlie Manuel won the Most Valuable Player award while playing for what team?

380. What Cleveland Cavalier was cleared of point-shaving gambling charges at his alma mater, Tulane University?

376. *Sandy Alomar, who singled in the bottom of the eighth inning to break up a no-hitter by Seattle pitcher Randy Johnson.*

377. *Jimmy Doyle.*

378. *John Havlicek. "Hondo" started out as a wide receiver with the Browns and ended his sports career as a guard with the Boston Celtics.*

379. *The 1979 Kinetsu Buffaloes of the Japanese major leagues.*

380. *John "Hot Rod" Williams.*

???

381. Who is the father of Cleveland's Metropark system?

382. What name did former Cleveland Indians outfielder Albert Belle go by during his early years with the Tribe (1989–1992)?

383. What two out-of-town college football teams played each other 11 times at Cleveland Municipal Stadium between 1932 and 1978?

384. What golf pro from Brecksville, Ohio's Sleepy Hollow Golf Course was the first black professional to win a PGA Tour event?

385. What prevented the Cleveland Indians from winning the American League pennant in 1918?

381. *William Stinchcomb, who directed the creation of the Cleveland-area park system beginning in 1917, when construction of public golf courses, bridle trails, hiking paths, and picnic areas began.*

382. *Joey, his middle name; he changed his name to Albert (his first name) after he completed alcohol rehab.*

383. *University of Notre Dame and the U.S. Naval Academy.*

384. *Charlie Sifford, who was the pro at Sleepy Hollow from 1975 to 1988, won the 1967 Hartford Open.*

385. *The draft. When U.S. Secretary of War Newton D. Baker ordered male citizens engaged in "non-essential" work to comply with the military draft on September 1, major league baseball ended its season with the Indians only 2 ½ games behind the faltering Boston Red Sox and closing in fast.*

386. Who was named starting quarterback for the Browns after Bernie Kosar was released in November, 1993?

387. What men's pro golf tournament was hosted at Highland Golf Course, Aurora Country Club, and Lakewood Country Club in its thirteen-year history from 1963 to 1975?

388. What record-breaking slugger did the Indians trade to the Kansas City Athletics in 1958 for Woody Held and Vic Power?

389. Who said "It's not that I love Cleveland less, but that I love Los Angeles more"? (Hint: 1946)

390. Who has played in the most games for the Cavaliers?

386. *Todd Philcox.*

387. *The Cleveland Open.*

388. *Roger Maris. Kansas City eventually dealt him to the Yankees, where he broke Babe Ruth's single-season home run record with 61 in 1961.*

389. *Dan Reeves, owner of the Cleveland Rams, about moving his NFL team to Los Angeles.*

390. *Bobby "Bingo" Smith, with 720 games.*

391. Name the three Cleveland sports teams that won championships in 1948.

392. In what park do the Akron Aeros play?

393. Who said "If I'm wrong about this man, I should consider getting out of football"? About whom did he say it?

394. In what sport did the Cleveland Buckeyes compete?

395. Name the Florida Marlins player whose hit off Indians pitcher Charlie Nagy in the eleventh inning of Game 7 of the 1997 World Series scored the winning run, giving the Marlins the world championship.

391. *The Indians won the World Series in major league baseball; the Browns won the All-America Football Conference championship; and the Cleveland Barons won the Calder Cup, the trophy for the American Hockey League champion.*

392. *Canal Park.*

393. *Art Modell, about his new head coach, Bill Belichick.*

394. *Baseball. The Buckeyes were the last of several Cleveland baseball teams to play in the Negro baseball leagues during the 1930s and 1940s. They went out of business after the 1948 season.*

395. *Edgar Renteria.*

???

396. Which local university played the first collegiate football game at Cleveland Municipal Stadium?

397. For what is Cleveland's Canterbury Country Club named?

398. Indians pitcher Dennis Martinez (1994–1996) was given this nickname by his 1995 Tribe teammates because of his political involvement in his native Nicaragua.

399. What Browns defensive tackle of the 1960s was known as "Little Mo"?

400. Who is the Cleveland Cavaliers' all-time leading scorer?

396. *John Carroll University. On September 24, 1931, JCU defeated Adrian College (Michigan), 26–6. The Blue Streaks called the Stadium home through 1935 and often played home games there through 1951.*

397. *Canterbury, Connecticut, birthplace of Moses Cleaveland.*

398. *El Presidente.*

399. *Dick Modzelewski (1964–1966), the younger brother of former Browns player Ed Modzelewski.*

400. *Brad Daugherty (1986-1994), with 10,389 points.*

???

401. What Bedford native had aces in the 1978 and 1982 U. S. Open tournaments?

402. Name the Cleveland artist who created the original Chief Wahoo caricature in 1947 at the request of Indians owner Bill Veeck.

403. What Browns 1987 first-round draft pick was described as "a mad dog in a meat market"?

404. Ernest Pflueger of Akron changed the sport of fishing with what invention?

405. Who sponsors the annual Cleveland triathalon?

401. *Tom Weiskopf. His feat still stands as a U.S. Golf Association record.*

402. *Walter Goldbach.*

403. *Mike Junkin, linebacker from Duke University.*

404. *Artificial bait and plugs (lures), helping revolutionize the sport.*

405. *National City Bank.*

? ?

406. Who wrote the *Plain Dealer* football column "Extra Points"?

407. What is Vulture's Knob?

408. What two former Indians players have palindromes (spelled the same forward and backward) for last names?

409. Who said "I had no choice!"? (1995)

410. What Cleveland State University basketball player was the first pick of the Philadelphia 76ers in the 1981 NBA draft?

406. Chuck Heaton.

407. A brutal three-mile mountain-bike course located west of Wooster.

408. Toby Harrah (1979–1983) and Dave Otto (1991–1992).

409. Art Modell, on why he moved the Browns franchise to Baltimore at the end of the 1995 season.

410. Franklin Edwards.

411. What was the first sporting event held at Cleveland's Public Auditorium?

412. Which Indians player slept with the lights on because he was afraid of ghosts?

413. Name the team that represented Cleveland in the indoor Arena Football League.

414. Which high school won its 15th Division I state wrestling title in 1999?

415. At various times it has been claimed that the Cleveland Indians were named in 1915 in honor of the first American Indian to play major league baseball. What was his name?

411. *Professional basketball between the New York Celtics and the Cleveland Rosenblums. The Celtics beat the Rosenblums by a score of 28–24 in 1923.*

412. *Chico Salmon.*

413. *The Cleveland Thunderbolts.*

414. *St. Edward High School of Lakewood.*

415. *Louis Francis Sockalexis.*

416. What did Hiram College, a former Browns training camp site, call the three Browns player reunions it sponsored in 1996, 1997, and 1999 while the team was on its hiatus?

417. The Richfield Coliseum, home of the Cleveland Cavaliers and Crusaders, opened in 1974 with what event?

418. What Cleveland suburb hosted a major league baseball game in 1902?

419. What *Cleveland Press* sports editor (1939–1958) was nicknamed "Whitey"?

420. Name the only Cleveland State University basketball player to play for the Cleveland Cavaliers.

416. *"The Boys Are Back in Town."*

417. *A Frank Sinatra concert.*

418. *Fairview Park. The Cleveland Broncos (formerly the Blues) played there on June 8, 1902, because the city of Cleveland had outlawed Sunday major league games.*

419. *Franklin Lewis.*

420. *Darren Tillis.*

? ?

421. This *Plain Dealer* sports editor once commented on the popularity of Cleveland professional wrestling, "Rasslin' (is) not a sport but a superbly staged act." Who said it?

422. What was the name of the Cleveland Indians' mascot before Slider?

423. Name the father and son who both performed play-by-play duties for Browns broadcasts in different eras.

424. How many acres of land does the Cuyahoga Valley National Recreational Area between Cleveland and Akron contain? A) 8,000; B) 17,000; C)33,000.

425. What is the name of the Cleveland Indians Class AAA minor league team in Buffalo, New York?

421. *Gordon Cobbledick.*

422. *Tom-E-Hawk was the birdlike mascot of the 1983–1985 seasons.*

423. *Ken Coleman and son Casey Coleman. Ken called the action on radio in 1952–1953, then switched to television from 1954 to 1965. Casey was the Browns radio voice in 1994–1995.*

424. *C) 33,000.*

425. *The Bisons.*

426. Who is the career leading scorer for the Cleveland Crunch?

427. In 1984, the world's top 12 women professional golfers met in Cleveland to compete in which tournament?

428. In addition to playing for the Indians, what do baseball greats Frank Robinson and Larry Doby have in common?

429. After he was fired as head coach of the Cleveland Browns in January 1963, what football team did Paul Brown coach beginning in 1968?

430. Where is the Ohio Derby held?

426. *Hector Marinaro.*

427. *The Chevrolet World Championship of Women's Golf.*

428. *They were the first two black managers in major league baseball, Robinson for the Cleveland Indians in 1975 and Doby for the Chicago White Sox in 1978.*

429. *The Cincinnati Bengals.*

430. *Thistledown Race Track in North Randall.*

???

431. The Cleveland Browns football team began play as a professional team in 1946. In what sport did the Cleveland Browns of 1924 compete?

432. What are the retired uniform numbers for the Cleveland Indians, and who wore them?

433. The Browns had two quarterbacks named Graham. What were their first names?

434. Which Cleveland pro sports team reached the playoffs in 1982, 1983, 1985, and 1986?

435. What Tribe third baseman made two spectacular defensive plays to help stop Joe DiMaggio's 56-game hitting streak?

431. Baseball. (Negro Baseball League.)

432. #3–Earl Averill, #5–Lou Boudreau, #14–Larry Doby, #18–Mel Harder, #19–Bob Feller, and #21–Bob Lemon. Note: Jackie Robinson's number, 42, is retired for every major league team.

433. Otto and Jeff. Hall of Fame quarterback Otto Graham played for the Browns from 1946 to 1955 and is recognized as one of the greatest quarterbacks to have played the game. The second Graham, Jeff, was a back-up quarterback for the Browns in 1989.

434. The Cleveland Force.

435. Ken Keltner.

? ?

436. Two Browns players later served as head coach of the team. Name them.

437. What local businessman created a wrestling dynasty at Lakewood's St. Edward High School?

438. In addition to hitting baseballs with them, what did the 1917 Cleveland Indians use their bats for in the year the U. S. entered World War I?

439. What Cleveland weatherman served as the official statistician for the Cleveland Browns' radio broadcast team?

440. Ted Stepien, owner of the Cleveland Cavaliers from 1980 to 1983, had a special name for the team's cheerleaders. What was it?

436. *Dick Modzelewski and Jim Shofner. Modzelewski, defensive tackle from 1964 to 1966, coached the final game of the Browns' 1977 season after head coach Forrest Gregg was fired. Shofner, defensive back from 1958 to 1963, held the reins for seven games in the 1990 season following the firing of coach Bud Carson.*

437. *Howard Ferguson.*

438. *As substitutes for rifles. At the urging of major league baseball, all teams were assigned army drill instructors to teach players how to march in formation—with bats instead of rifles.*

439. *Dick Goddard.*

440. *The "Teddy Bears."*

???

441. What international tennis match was hosted in Cleveland ten times between 1960 and 1979?

442. Who said "Pennant fever in Cleveland is usually a twenty-four-hour virus"?

443. In the 1980s, Cleveland had a team in the Women's Professional Football League. What was the team's name?

444. Match the area high school with its athletic team name:
    1. Hudson   a. Mustangs
    2. Bay Village   b. Arcs
    3. Maple Heights   c. Bombers
    4. Brush   d. Explorers
    5. Kenston   e. Rockets

445. Who were the "Big Four"?

441. *The Davis Cup. Six preliminary matches and four championship finals were played here.*

442. *Frank Robinson, Indians manager (1975–1977).*

443. *The Cleveland Brewers.*

444. *1 (d), 2 (e), 3 (a), 4 (b), 5 (c).*

445. *Indians starting pitchers Bob Lemon, Early Wynn, Bob Feller, and Mike Garcia, who combined for 367 victories between 1950 and 1954.*

446. Cleveland sports personality Les Levine is famous for what question-and-answer game?

447. The 1946 Masters Golf Tournament champion hailed from Akron. Who is he?

448. What was the nickname of Indians pitcher Wayne Garland (1977–1981)?

449. From which college have the Browns drafted prospective players most frequently?

450. Where did the Cleveland Cavaliers' first coach, Bill Fitch, acquire the information he used to select players from other NBA teams when assembling his first team in 1970?

446. The "How come quickie."

447. Herman Kaiser.

448. The "Two Million Dollar Man." In 1977, Garland signed a 10-year, $2.3 million contract with the Tribe.

449. Ohio State University.

450. From bubblegum trading cards.

??

451. Who was the original radio voice of the Cavaliers?

452. Name the Cleveland-born third baseman who played in three World
     Series with the Oakland Athletics. (His brother played for the Indians
     from 1981 to 1988.)

453. Name the uniform numbers that are no longer issued to players by the
     Cleveland Browns, and the players who wore them.

454. What was the last event held at the Richfield Coliseum?

455. Name the Indians catcher who caught three no-hitters from three sepa-
     rate Tribe pitchers. While you're at it, name the three pitchers, too.

451. Joe Tait.

452. Sal Bando. Sal's brother Chris was a catcher for the Tribe.

453. #14, Otto Graham QB (1946–1955); #32, Jim Brown FB (1957–1965); #46, Ernie Davis HB (1962, did not play); #46, Don Fleming DB (1960–1962); and #76, Lou Groza OT/PK (1946–1959; 1961–1967).

454. A Roger Daltry concert in 1994.

455. Catcher Jim Hegan (1941–1942; 1946–1957) caught no-hitters by Don Black (1947), Bob Lemon (1948), and Bob Feller (1951).

? ?

456. After winning the 1945 National Football League Championship, Cleveland's football team moved to what city?

457. Clevelander Edward Henning was the oldest candidate for the Sullivan Award, given to the country's outstanding amateur athlete. In what sport did Henning compete?

458. Which Indian broke into the umpires' dressing room at Comiskey Park to steal Albert Belle's corked bat and prevent it from being examined?

459. Who holds the Browns' record for longest run from scrimmage?

460. How many Cleveland-area high-school basketball players have won the Ohio "Mr. Basketball" award since its inception in 1988?

456. *The Cleveland Rams moved west to Los Angeles, California.*

457. *Gymnastics. Henning finished third in the Sullivan balloting at age 62 in 1942. Henning went on to win a gymnastics tournament at age 71.*

458. *Pitcher Jason Grimsley.*

459. *Halfback Bobby Mitchell, who ran 90 yards for a touchdown against the Washington Redskins on November 15, 1959.*

460. *Three. Damon Stringer, Cleveland Heights (1995); Sonny Johnson, Garfield Heights (1998); Emmanuel Smith, Euclid (1999). The award goes to the best prep basketballer in the state.*

461. The Alcazar, a historic Cleveland Heights hotel, hosts a local sporting club of the same name. What sport?

462. How did Indians general manager Frank Lane refer to fan favorite Rocky Colavito, whom he traded away to the Detroit Tigers before the start of the 1960 season?

463. In 1984, what organization was formed to aid the activities of Cleveland Browns fan clubs?

464. The winner of this *Plain Dealer* contest for teens between the ages of 13 and 17 won summer employment and a scholarship. What was it?

465. How many brother combinations have played together for the Cleveland Indians since 1920? Name them.

461. *Fencing. (The Alcazar Fencing Club, founded in 1977, has produced two Olympic champions—Steve Trevor in 1984 and 1988, and Jon Normile in 1992.)*

462. *Lane called Rocky a "handsome fruit peddler." Cleveland fans would have loved to peddle some fruit at Lane after the trade.*

463. *The Browns Backers.*

464. *The* Plain Dealer *Bat Boy Contest, which ran from the late 1940s to the early 1970s.*

465. *Three. Joe and Luke Sewell (1921–1930); Jim and Gaylord Perry (1974–75); Sandy and Roberto Alomar (1999–). (Dick and Larry Brown both played for the Indians, but not during the same seasons.)*

466. How many times have the Cleveland Browns won the National Football
     League Championship game? Who were their opponents?

467. The Cleveland Arena hosted what 1952 event that helped popularize the
     term "rock 'n' roll"?

468. What Indians infielder made the last out in the last game played at
     Municipal Stadium on October 3, 1993?

469. What was The Inner Circle?

470. What was the nickname of the flashy college basketball player Kevin
     McFadden, who played for CSU during the mid-1980s?

466. *Four. 1950, L.A. Rams; 1954, Detroit Lions; 1955, L.A. Rams; 1964, Baltimore Colts.*

467. *The first Moondog Coronation Ball, promoted by disc jockey Alan Freed.*

468. *Shortstop Mark Lewis struck out.*

469. *A drug-addiction intervention group formed by the Browns for their players in the early 1980s. It served as a model for other pro sports teams.*

470. *Kevin "Mouse" McFadden (he played guard).*

471. What honor was bestowed upon 79-year-old Clevelander Jimmy Bivens on January 12, 1999?

472. What Indians player appeared in the 1984 movie *The Natural*, which starred Robert Redford as baseball phenom Roy Hobbs?

473. Which former University of Notre Dame head coach played for the Browns in 1948–1949?

474. Where did the Cleveland Barons play before the Cleveland Arena opened in 1937?

475. Who sang the National Anthem before Indians home games from 1974 to 1993?

471. *He was inducted into the International Boxing Hall of Fame. (Bivens's ring record was 86 wins, 25 defeats, 1 draw with 31 knockouts between 1940 and 1955.)*

472. *Joe Charboneau, 1980 Rookie of the Year.*

473. *Ara Parseghian.*

474. *The Elysium Ice Rink on Euclid Avenue at 107th Street.*

475. *Rocco Scotti.*

??

476. What John Hay High School alumnus and Ohio State Buckeye won the NFL's 1974 Rookie of the Year award as an offensive lineman with the New York Giants?

477. Where did the Cleveland Barons hockey team move after their final season in Cleveland in 1973?

478. Who was named the Most Valuable Player of major league baseball's 1997 All-Star Game played in Cleveland on July 8, 1997?

479. What was the title of Jim Brown's 1964 autobiography?

480. What were the Cavaliers' original team colors?

476. *John Hicks.*

477. *Jacksonville, Florida.*

478. *Sandy Alomar, who hit the game-winning home run in the seventh inning to give the American League a 3–1 victory over the National League.*

479. *Off My Chest.*

480. *Wine and gold.*

481. Who has the most Cleveland Grand Prix auto race victories since the race's inception in 1982?

482. Which team has beaten the Indians the most times since 1915?

483. What Mayfield High School and Ohio State University football player was selected as a Rhodes Scholar in 1985?

484. What organization touts itself as the "snowboarding capital of Ohio"?

485. What Garfield Heights, Ohio, native is remembered for making the only unassisted triple play in World Series history?

481. *Danny Sullivan and Emerson Fittipaldi have both won the event three times.*

482. *The New York Yankees.*

483. *Mike Lanese.*

484. *The Boston Mills-Brandywine Ski Areas in Peninsula.*

485. *Bill "Wamby" Wambsganss accomplished this feat as a member of the Cleveland Indians in the 1920 World Series.*

???

486. What description did radio station WHK AM apply to their broadcasts of Cleveland Browns games in the 1960s and 1970s?

487. Lakewood's Timothy Goebel was the first to perform what jump, during the men's world figure-skating competition in March 1999?

488. What is the title of 1946–1949 Cleveland Indians owner Bill Veeck's biography?

489. What caused the death of Browns safety Don Rogers in 1986?

490. What was the name of Cleveland's 1925–26 professional basketball team that won the American Basketball League title?

486. *"The greatest show in football."*

487. *The quadruple salchow.*

488. Veeck As in Wreck.

489. *A cocaine overdose.*

490. *The Cleveland Rosenblums. Owned by Max Rosenblum, a local clothing-store magnate, the team defeated the Brooklyn Arcadians for the championship.*

CLEVELAND SPORTS TRIVIA QUIZ **Q** ▶

? ?

491.   Name the legendary high-school coach who led Maple Heights High
       School to ten state championships and a 265–25 dual wrestling meet
       record from 1950 to 1977.

492.   Jim Leyritz, the 1996 New York Yankee catcher who helped the Bronx
       Bombers win the World Series that year, was born in what West Side
       Cleveland suburb?

493.   What was the name of the professional soccer team that played home
       games at Municipal Stadium in the 1970s?

494.   Which public golf course features Federal Aviation Administration (FAA)
       control equipment right on the course?

495.   In 1960, Indians general manager Frank Lane traded Joe Gordon to the
       Detroit Tigers for Jimmy Dykes. What was unusual about this transac-
       tion?

491. *Mike Milkovich.*

492. *Lakewood.*

493. *The Cleveland Cobras.*

494. *Airport Greens Golf Course in Willoughby.*

495. *Gordon and Dykes were the managers of their respective ball clubs.*

? ?

496. What tabloid publication of the Cleveland Browns would one have been reading for the first time at the start of the 1981 football season?

497. For what Cleveland sports team did Martina Navratilova play?

498. Name the American League umpire who ejected both Indians manager Mike Hargrove and pitcher Dwight Gooden in the first inning of game 2 of the 1998 division playoffs against the Boston Red Sox.

499. What was the name of the first movie in which Cleveland Browns fullback Jim Brown appeared?

500. What local Catholic men's organization sponsored indoor track meets in the 1950s, '60s, and '70s at the former Cleveland Arena and the Richfield Coliseum?

496. *Browns News Illustrated.*

497. *The Cleveland Nets professional tennis team.*

498. *Joe Brinkman. The ejections proved a spark for the Tribe as they went on to win the game and the playoff series from the Red Sox.*

499. *Rio Conchos. (Brown appeared in the western while still an active player.)*

500. *The Knights of Columbus.*